Dynamics
of
Success

TORKOM SARAYDARIAN

T.S.G.
PUBLISHING FOUNDATION

Visions for the Twenty-First Century®

Dynamics of Success

ISBN: 0-929874-26-9

Library of Congress Catalog Number 91-91402

Printed in the United States of America

Cover design: *Fine Point Graphics*
                  Sedona, Arizona

Printed by: *Thomson - Shore, Inc.*
                  Dexter, Michigan

Published by: **T.S.G. Publishing Foundation, Inc.**
                  Visions for the Twenty-First Century
                  P.O. Box 4273
                  West Hills, California 91308
                  United States of America

Note: The exercises contained in this book are given as guidelines. They should be used with discretion and after receiving professional advice.

Table of Contents

A Few Words

The business community is beginning to recognize something it has intuitively felt for a long time: that success does not mean financial gain alone; that business must yield emotional, mental, and spiritual prosperity for all men everywhere in the world. The fact has finally emerged that the root cause of failure is separativeness and the pursuit of individual success at the expense of others.

In *The Spring of Prosperity* Torkom Saraydarian stated that true prosperity is the abundance in our life of virtues, health, and friends, as well as money. Nature is abundance itself, and man has that same treasury within him. Since the publishing of that book, the author has been asked what are the secrets of success, and how can a person be very successful in life and still remain loving, kind, and caring.

In *Dynamics of Success* Torkom Saraydarian provides a comprehensive and multidimensional look at success. He states that to achieve success, we must approach life in an integrated manner: We need to fulfill the physical and material requirements and also the spiritual qualities, *and* we need to eliminate all hindrances in our life that prevent our success.

Success is an integral part of prosperity. It is in our highest interest and in the interest of humanity to know how to be successful and prosperous in life without the violation of the fundamental laws of Nature.

People have the idea that being a successful person automatically means that one is not a decent person. This is not true. In order to benefit ourselves, as well as gain ever inclusive benefits for humanity, it is essential that we train ourselves and our children *how* to find a job, keep it, and succeed in it; and *how* to instill the right values and right motives, *how* to be truly successful, and *how* to find the purpose of life.

To move ahead in life and to insure our global survival we need the right values, practically applied. *Dynamics of Success* presents practical and easy to follow guidelines on the road to success in your career and your life.

Apply and practice the ideas in this book and see how you and all those around you will have success — which is true direction, abundance, and prosperity.

— The Publisher —

Chapter 1

What is Success?

Most human beings have the urge to be successful because success leads to survival and to the enjoyment of life.

In our daily life and in our particular field of work or labor there are many steps that can be taken to secure our success in our home, work, society, and in the field of our many relationships.

Success has two wings. There is spiritual success; there is material success. You are going to find the balance between these two successes. If you become very successful spiritually and not physically or materially, you are out of balance. If you lose yourself within physical success, you are out of balance. Sometimes people sell their souls to be very successful financially, materially, or physically, but they lose their higher goals and the purpose of their life.

If the two phases of one reality are not balanced in your life, you cannot be considered a successful person. You are going to be growing like a tree. Your roots must have good soil, and you must have good space around you. This space must not be polluted, but it must have sunshine and energies from stars and constellations that will nourish your soul. Your physical life must be balanced with energies coming from Space.

> *Every success starts from a point of balance.*

Everyone of you who wants to be successful in your life is going to watch these two processes. You must be physically successful — have money, health, a home, clothing, and all that you need to be happy. But all these things will work against your ultimate success if you do not have spiritual success.

What is spiritual success? You are going to deepen your sensitivity, increase your knowledge of the natural laws, purify your heart, organize your mind, and build those bridges that put you in contact with higher sources of energy and knowledge.

Spiritual success is the actualization of your inner potentials and of your essential divinity through your thoughts, feelings, words, and actions. A spiritual man develops a sense of unity with all living forms in Nature and tries to help them without any selfish expectations.

When you have both spiritual success and material success, you will have balance in your life; and when you have balance, you will have true success. *Every success starts from a point of balance.* That is a very important statement, and if you approach the problems in your life from that viewpoint, then you will try to balance your life before you step into a greater success.

Suppose an airplane breaks one of its wings in mid-flight. It can no longer fly. It goes a little distance and falls. The same thing happens with us. We must be materially and physically up-to-date, and then we must increase our spiritual wealth before we can be a success. Failure starts when one of these sides falls short.

How can you achieve spiritual success? There are six things that are very important to do:

1. *Expand your consciousness* because in expanding your consciousness you can see your physical obstacles, hindrances, possibilities, and opportunities. This is the physical side. In expanding your consciousness you can also see the kinds of energies, ideas, visions, and revelations that you need in order to make your physical success possible. Then you will be able to use your physical success as a device to manifest your spiritual wealth.

When your consciousness expands it does two things. It penetrates into your physical mechanism, your physical life, and tries to organize that life in such a way that your physical success becomes possible. Then your consciousness penetrates into the laws of Nature, ideas, visions, and inspirations and uses them to make your physical life successful.

But when your physical life is successful, that life is not going to work for itself; it is going to be a tool, a device to manifest the visions of your spiritual success. In this way you expand with two wings and move ahead because your two wings move you forward physically and spiritually.

When you expand your consciousness, you bring balance and equilibrium into your life. You balance the physical wing with the spiritual wing and make them serve each other instead of serving themselves. That is why we see many, many rich people or very successful people who suddenly vanish or fall from their heights due to health problems, moral problems, family problems, or divorce problems. All these things happen because the spiritual side and the physical side were not in good balance.

Real success is like your brain; it has a left side and a right side. They must be balanced. When they are balanced, you have a better life. When your two feet are balanced, you have a better walk. The first point in obtaining success in your life is to concentrate on the idea that your life will not be a one track life. Your life will be balanced between both the spiritual and the physical sides of your nature. If you introduce this fact into your daily affairs, you will become more and more successful.

Expansion of consciousness can be achieved by

    a. Studying all that is related to your job

    b. Looking at your job from the viewpoint of

        — service

        — income

        — all those who are related to your job

    c. Thinking how your job can help people be healthy, happy, and prosperous

    d. Having an interest in new scientific discoveries and political events

2. *Expand your spirituality.* Spirituality is translated in certain writings as religion. It is not. Spirituality has nothing to do with religion. Spirituality means continuous advancement, progress, and expansion of your ideas, of your efforts, of your service. When being spiritual, you are expanding your knowledge, your ideas, your visions, your plans, your field of service; you are going toward success. You cannot advance spiritually unless you take both of your sides into consideration and develop both of them. For example, a man is not

really spiritual if he retreats in the forest for his own salvation and remains there without helping humanity. A man is not spiritual if he is making millions of dollars but not contributing to the spiritualization of humanity.

Spirituality, like consciousness, must work for both sides of your nature. On one side, spirituality makes you successful, healthier, more beautiful, and makes your relationships with others better. On the other side, spirituality helps your mind to advance, your soul to bloom, and your inner hidden faculties to reveal and actualize themselves.

People who are balanced between matter and spirit can be useful for mankind and are considered successful.

People are spiritual when they work for their financial and physical affairs and put them in order and, at the same time, try to advance their mind and spirit and build a better relationship with the higher forces of Nature.

Spirituality means advancing from both sides, unfolding and flowering. We must have a generation in the future that is not totally lost in matter. Also, we must not have a generation that is totally abstracted and spaced out. People who are balanced between matter and spirit can be useful for mankind and are considered successful.

If a scientist is working in the field of chemistry or physics and he is totally lost in it, he is not balanced and he may create atomic bombs or other destructive weapons. He is going to create those kinds of inventions that are going to hurt your health and happiness on this earth. But if that scientist has developed his spiritual side, he will have a balance in his creativity. He will ask, "If I am creating this device, is it going to serve humanity or is it going to create problems and pollution and destruction?"

By the same token, if you are going to choose a girlfriend or boyfriend or get married, you must use discrimination. Discrimination is the result of an outlook that considers both the physical and spiritual factors and reaches a balanced conclusion. Some people choose their boyfriend or girlfriend because he or she is rich or physically looks beautiful and healthy, but they seldom ask about the spirituality of the person. "Is he spiritual or is she spiritual? Does he have great vision? Is she noble? Is she trustworthy, helpful, sacrificial? Does he or she have a sense of responsibility?" These are the spiritual sides of the relationship.

If you go to the beach and see a beautiful leg and you marry the leg, you have a problem because you must also take the other leg! This is very practical for us, and in every approach of our life, we are going to see both sides. This business, this man, this woman, this book, this lecture: Is there balance in them? Do they have both sides of their life balanced or are they fanatic and dedicated to only one field, neglecting and ignoring the other field that exists to balance their life.

3. *Try always to have the Law of Karma behind you.* Karma is the Law of Cause and Effect. All action in physical, emotional, and mental realms creates reaction. Action and reaction balance themselves in your life. Your life is the result of the seeds of actions. Sometimes you do everything physically possible, spiritually possible, but still you are not successful. What is the factor that prevents your success? The factor is your bad karma. Why do you have bad karma? In the past you did not throw good seeds on the earth and now you are expecting the best harvest, but there is no good harvest because you did not plant good seeds in the ground.

...to be successful in the future, you must make other people successful now.

Knowing this, you gain great wisdom. In this wisdom you learn that *to be successful in the future, you must make other people successful now.* Politics, economy, finance, even science has never considered the karmic part of success. You will never enjoy your success, even if you are a genius, if your karma does not tolerate you to go ahead because in the past you did not sow the seeds for future successes.

The moral lesson in this is that now, at the present, you must do everything possible to secure the success of others so that you can have future success.

Karma works in every direction. Let us say that you are a medical doctor. You have everything possible to make yourself healthy, but you are unhealthy. You are striving to be healthy, but you cannot be healthy because your karma is not tolerating you to be healthy. Why is that? This occurs because in the past you made others unhealthy. You planted so many causes that made other people unhealthy. Now you are reaping the effects of what you did in the past to others.

You take a book and you really want to understand and learn from that book and really practice it. For example, you take *The Purpose of Life*[1] and you say to me, "What a nice book this is. What beautiful things are given in that book — ideas, visions, laws, rules, great plans, great inspiration." Okay, wonderful! The book is good. You read it and read it, but you cannot practice it because something is stopping you from practicing or actualizing the contents. What is happening? In the past you prevented people from being spiritual, practical, and self-actualized. Now, no matter what you do, you cannot be successful even in understanding that book, even sometimes in

---

1. *The Purpose of Life*, by Torkom Saraydarian.

buying the book, even in having money to go to a seminar. Something is preventing you, and that something is your past karma.

For our success we need not only expansion of consciousness, we need not only spirituality, but we also need karma that is not an obstacle. The lack of karmic obstacles is like having a wind behind us. We were once flying from Europe to New York. The pilot told us, "We have a one hundred eighty miles per hour wind at our tail." As a result, we were to arrive two hours early.

Having the Law of Karma behind you is just like that. It is like entering into the jet stream which takes you to success, and you wonder why this success is coming to you. You had sowed the right seeds in the past.

We cannot *quickly change* our past; therefore we must concentrate on the present. To make our life successful for the future, we must make the lives of other people successful financially and spiritually. This is the opportunity for all of us to make ourselves successful in the future.

But how can we overcome the results of our past karma and pave the way for our success? The answer is as follows:

> a. Try to understand that your present failure is rooted in the way you lived your life in the past.

b. Try to help people live in a way that *you* want to live in the future.

4. *Be honest.* This is the fourth factor for spiritual success. Honesty is one of the keys to success. The more honest and balanced you are with yourself and with others — with yourself and with your boss, with yourself and with your business, with yourself and with your vision — the more successful you will be because honesty and balance attract all those creative forces in the Universe that help you become successful. Success as a result of dishonesty eventually fails because it loses its magnetism and disintegrates. But honesty creates that magnetism within you, within your group, and within your environment that attracts all those creative forces that are going to make you truly successful.

What does it mean to be honest with yourself? To be honest with yourself means not to deceive yourself, not to cover up for yourself, but to face yourself from A to Z. For example, if it is your mistake, admit it. If you caused things to happen destructively, accept it. Be frank, sincere, and open; be honest with yourself.

Be honest with other people because your honesty will not increase and expand until your honesty is reflected and related to the life you have with others. If you are honest with yourself but not honest with your husband or wife, you destroy your balance.

Honesty is also the ability to work on spiritual and physical fields simultaneously.

What is balance? Balance is the ability to keep the demands of your life proportionate to each other and to create a condition in which your giving and taking fit the container you have.

The elements of life are the physical body and physical forms, the emotional body and emotions, the mental body and thoughts, and the spiritual bodies and their virtues. Your actions in any of these areas must be the result of the balance of all these elements.

5. *Grow in nobility.* Nobility means self-respect, righteous living, and a righteous attitude. A noble person does not manipulate and exploit others. A noble person helps to make Beauty, Goodness, Righteousness, Joy, and Freedom increase. A noble person is sacrificial.

> *The more love you have, the more success you will have...*

6. *Increase your love.* People think that hatred brings success. People think that separatism brings success. People think that if you rob other people, you become successful. If you live a life at the expense of others, they call it being successful. But the laws of Nature work in different ways. The more love you have, the more success you will have — a success that is going to continue forever and expand forever. Your individual politics with people, your individual relationships with people must be based on love.

What is love? Love is the spirit to create right human relations with people wherever you are, in whatever business you are, and it means to care for people. For example, take a girl who works in an office but hates her boss or co-workers. That girl is not going to last in the office too long because she is working against the principles of success. What are the principles of success? ...Consciousness, spirituality, karma, honesty, nobility, and love.

Love means to be inclusive, to make yourself understood, and to understand other people. In this way your love will make everything possible for you and for others to be successful.

These six spiritual factors will naturally create within you the ability to draw money, knowledge, find the right location, the right environment, the right job, and the right timing to make it all possible.

Love means to be in- clusive, to make your- self under- stood, and to under- stand other people.

People try to have success, but the material success is a source of suffering and pain if it is not the result of spiritual success. When the six powers are cultivated in men and women, it will be impossible for success not to follow their steps.

Chapter 2

Factors for Success

There are other factors which will help to bring you more success.

You must work hard to know all about the field in which you are going to work. How can you be an electrician without learning about it? Or how can you be a violinist without practicing at least three hours a day for it?

You need to study the location where you will work. Check this location from the viewpoint of psychological effects, as well as from the viewpoint of business and health. You must discover the right environment which will encourage and inspire you and will help you be successful.

You must search for the right job you fit into.

You need right timing — for your maturity, and for making your job application.

Of course, astrologers can give you much advice regarding the right timing, but remember that you have a more complicated instrument within you that is far superior to astrology; that is your heart. Try to use your heart as the closest adviser in your job and in your decisions.[1]

...our success must be the result of our own labor and right motives.

Another factor in our success is the awareness that our success must be the result of our own labor and right motives.

People blame others for their failures and then create more obstacles on the path of their success.

We must know that most of the time the cause of our failures is found within us. This is very important to understand. Unless you depend on yourself and use all your resources to succeed, you will never be successful.

---

1. For additional information, please see *The Flame of the Heart.*

Success is the fruit of your labor. Failure is the result of many past and present wrong attitudes and actions.

Whenever you fail, do not condemn others for various reasons and in various ways. Instead, search for the causes of failure within you. It is only by making such an effort that you will start to stand on your feet and take responsibility for your life.

Those who inherit success, if they are not worthy or ready for it, soon lose it. Do not expect people to help you. Do not exercise pressure on others to help you. Neither blame them nor be angry if they do not help you.

Sometimes to find ...causes of defeat is more important than your temporary success.

Start thinking that your success must be the result of your own efforts, labor, health, happiness, and intellignece. Whenever you fail, search for the reasons within you.

People may become successful with the help of others, but once the others vanish, the people fall into the path of defeat.

But remember that in failure you are not going to condemn even yourself but, instead, scientifically look for the causes. *Sometimes to find such causes of defeat is more important than your temporary success.*

Often your success lasts for a few years, but when you eliminate the causes of failure in you, your success becomes a continually growing adventure.

Depend on yourself and make your success the fruit of your own labor. Of course, do not forget that you must express gratitude to the Invisible Forces who helped you because you helped yourself.

Question & Answer

Question: *Can you explain how some spiritual people give more time for their spiritual work and less to their physical work, but have all that they need?*

Answer: We were told that Christ did not have any place to sleep, but very rich people opened their doors to have Him eat with them, sleep with them, feast with them, and dress the best. Everyone gave gifts that you cannot imagine. For example, the three Magi brought the most expensive gifts to Him. He had everything. He did not need many things.

Also, His physical body was perfect. He had perfect emotions and the purest thoughts. That was His physical side. Because He had everything else, He totally dedicated Himself to make people physically and spiritually prosperous.

If you minimize your artificial or imposed needs, you can have more resources to be successful. People like to build traps for themselves and be trapped in them.

Buddha did not have artificial and imposed needs. People say that Buddha did not have anything, but some powerful kings gave Him hundreds of acres of property, temples, buildings. He had everything. Why did He have them? ...Because He did not attach to those things that they gave Him.

It is a wrong idea to think that spirituality is not connected with prosperity. You need material things. You need the best car. You are a king. You are going to live in the best places, dress in the nicest clothes, have the nicest houses — *but not at the expense of your spirituality*. That is where you are going to pay attention. If your financial or physical things eat you, swallow you, you are finished. You must put in your mind that your whole physical environment is going to serve a great purpose, and that great purpose must be spiritual. You must strive toward sublimation and transformation of your life.[2]

> **Question:** *If the path of your career takes you one way and the path of your spiritual vision takes you another way, how do you find the balance between them?*

Answer: This is what many people fail to understand. There will not be two ways. I will give you a very simple example. There was a nun in the Catholic Church who became a Saint. When she became a nun, they gave her the duty to wash the dirtiest clothes of the sick nuns and sick brothers. The clothes were

---

2. Please see *The Purpose of Life* and *The Spring of Prosperity*.

bloody, messy, and at that time they did not have machines to wash clothes. This poor girl had to wash them with her hands. The first day she was very angry because she thought, "I came to the monastery expecting great lectures, great visions, great ideas, inspirations, prayers, and singing. What is this? They gave me this mess, and here I am working each day with my hands to clean all this mess." She started to rebel against herself until one afternoon she went to church and prayed. A great idea came to her about how to make the washing of the dirty clothes spiritual. "Oh," she said, "I can assume that all these dirty clothes belong to Christ and I am washing His clothes." She became so joyful. Day and night she was washing the clothes and saying, "Jesus, you know I am washing these pants for You. These linens I am washing for You. These I am washing for You." She became more and more joyful. As she continued serving in joy, she started to see visions. Christ came and talked to her. Saints came and talked to her. Angels came and talked to her, and They gave better lectures than her seniors in the monastery.

It is a wrong idea to think that spirituality is not connected with prosperity.

If you do not make a division between spirituality and physical life, you can find the secret for success in your daily, smallest jobs. Dedicate that work for a great purpose. For example say, "I am writing this letter to this girl to make her more courageous, more beautiful, more pure, and if this girl becomes what I am dreaming her to be, then I am serving the Will of God, and when I am serving the Will of God, I am really spiritual because I am connected with the spiritual dynamo."

> *The ultimate goal of all our services is to make us realize that everything we do is really done for All.*

Never divide spirituality from life because everywhere you go, you meet spirit and matter. If you do not divide them, you can make matter spiritual and make spirit serve matter. The two serve each other in such a balanced way that you are able to move ahead physically and spiritually into a successful life.

Even if you are typing in your office, say, "I am typing this for Christ, for Buddha, for Krishna." You regret and you become rebellious against your daily duties and responsibilities because you think that you are doing this labor for a nobody or for the dollar you are receiving. It is there that you are missing your spirituality.

The ultimate goal of all our services is to make us realize that everything we do is really done for ALL. This is a major key for great success.

Chapter 3

The Three Sides of Success

Success is not limited to physical and spiritual prosperity. It has another facet that you must consider. If you eliminate in your life certain obstacles and problems and resistances, that is also a great success.

Success now has three sides. One side is physical, another side is spiritual, and the third side, which always creates friction with the two sides, is your hindrances, burdens, and attachments. What are you going to do? You are going to take the field of your service, the field of your business, the field of your family or social life *and find those obstacles and hindrances* that are preventing you from expanding, growing, and flourishing. That is very important because as long as you are looking from behind many hindrances, problems, and obstacles, they grow and then they run ahead of you and meet you at another crossroad on your path in the future.

Success... also must dissolve the problems that you have, the frictions that exist in your life.

With your physical success and spiritual success you must have also the success of eliminating the problems, misunderstandings, obstacles, and hindrances that you have within you, between you and others, and in the field of your service. That will guarantee your complete success. For example, if you see that you and your husband or wife have a little problem, an obstacle, a hindrance, or a misunderstanding, do not ignore it but try to solve it instead. If it remains unresolved, it will grow and become your tail. Success must make your physical and spiritual life beautiful, but it also must dissolve the problems that you have, the frictions that exist in your life. Unless you create an open space for yourself by solving your problems and obstacles, you cannot fly, you cannot proceed in your success, because every problem left unsolved will grow and create difficulties for your future advancement.

You have three kinds of jobs to do: prepare the physical side of your success, prepare the spiritual side of your success, and also eliminate your obstacles.

Sometimes you think that because one hundred people are not hating you, but only one person is hating you, it is okay. But that one person can be a factor for your many failures. You are going to solve that problem with your humility, with your understanding, your spirituality, your expanded consciousness, your nobility, your honesty, your sincerity. You are going to use any tool possible to dissolve obstacles, problems, and resistances and try to make, by all possible means, your enemies into your co-workers. That is the greatest success that eventually will

...try to make, by all possible means, your enemies into your co-workers.

be noticed by higher forces and they will say, "We are going to give you a secret of success because you tried to create cooperation."

Christ once said, "When you are going to bring your gifts to the altar and you are going to pray, first go and create understanding with your enemy and clear the animosity and then come and offer your gifts." But we do not do that. We say, "Others are very bad people, they are slanderers, they are gossipers, they are haters, they are revengeful people, so let them go to hell." But one who wants to be successful considers the effect of animosity, tries to eliminate it slowly, slowly, and tries to make his enemies serve the purpose that he is serving.

For example, some politicians wish to destroy a particular nation to make their own nation successful. Okay, that is one way. But if we are smarter we will make that nation our co-worker, our friend. Then we will have greater success. Politics is eventually going to change under these principles. Instead of killing, robbing, and destroying people, it is going to make them more prosperous and closer to each other in cooperation so that each of them reaches the ultimate purpose that everyone is working for.

One day a girl came to me and said, "I am sick all the time. I am not successful. I am failing in everything."

I said, "Do you have problems with your mother?"

"Oh," she said, "she is Satan. I hate her."

"Well," I said, "that is the cause of your failure."

"No, my mother does not have anything to do with my business."

"Well," I said, "you think so, but the problem you have with your mother is a problem in your consciousness; and if your consciousness has a tumor, that consciousness is not going to lead you to success. It is not outside; it is inside of you. What if you try to do something and find a better language between you and your mother and dissolve these problems?"

She did. She sent a card, then a gift, then gave her a radio and a television set. With three hundred dollars she won the heart of the mother. After the first time they hugged each other, the mother gave a gift of five thousand dollars. The daughter said, "I am successful!" That is success. Why be defeated by hatred?

We can defeat hatred. Of course these things are very easy to say, but they are not too easy to do because we have pride, vanity, and ego. Pride, vanity, and ego stand on our path and prevent us from taking those actions that will dissolve animosity.

If you forget to say hello to a girl, she says, "He is not even saying hello to me and he is like this and he is like that." You hear all she says and think, "Never mind." But her anger grows and grows and becomes animosity against you because you did not face the issue. But if you approach the problem and use your wisdom to destroy the problem, then it is possible to clear the misunderstanding, change her consciousness, and make her understand you and cooperate with you.

You will make great spiritual progress if you notice these few things.

Chapter 4

Six Factors to Eliminate for Success

To have success in your life, you must eliminate

— fear

— hatred

— slander

— treason

— jealousy

— revenge

One of the factors that you are going to eliminate from your life is **fear**. Fear is a parasite that comes and enters into your nervous system and paralyzes you. Try not to talk about fear, not to think about fear, not to make people afraid of you, and do not allow other people to plant fear in your heart. When fear is eliminated from your system, you have a great chance to be successful.

> *When you are fearless and balanced, you control the powers that are against you.*

Most people cannot have success because they have fears in them. But the law of Nature works in a different way. When you are fearless and balanced, you control the powers that are against you. Without fear, you become a very successful person. Fear can paralyze your nervous system, your efficiency, your striving. Any kind of fear that comes into your business, into your family life, into your children's lives, try to stop it because fear is a virus. To overcome fear is a great success in itself.

Remember that you must not act against any spiritual, moral, and social laws. Those who act against such laws are continuously chased by fear. There are many sources of fear; stop the sources and such fears will vanish.

The second factor to eliminate is **hatred**. Try as much as possible not to hate. What does hate do?

Hatred creates great disturbances in the symphony of your life's plan and in the purpose that you are conceiving in your consciousness. It burns the wires and takes the electricity out of your system. It really eats you, and when you are eaten by hatred, do not expect that you are going to be successful.

Then you will ask, "What about those people who are embodiments of hatred and they are successful?" They are not. They are the most miserable people. They have money, but they cannot enjoy it. They have wives, but until morning they fight with them. They have children, but they are miserable. They do not enjoy what they have. *When you do not enjoy what you have spiritually and physically, you are a failure.*

When you do not enjoy what you have spiritually and physically, you are a failure.

Hatred totally paralyzes your mechanism of success and makes you take actions that lead you toward disaster. If you learn these things, you will very soon be a successful person because you will eliminate these bugs from your system.

The third one to eliminate is **slander**. Do not be engaged in slander because it will create disturbances in your mind. It will burn the communication lines that you are building for your success. Success goes through communication. Communication is a great factor in success — communication through letters, through voice, through handshakes, through speeches. Your communication system is around you. But when you are engaged in slander, this system is burned in many places and is eventually destroyed and you become the victim of your own slander.

A slanderer buries himself in his own grave. Do not bury yourself in your self-made grave because you were created to be a successful person. If you have any problem with another, meet him and talk about it. If the problem is ten dollars, "Okay, half for you, half for me." It is over. Solve your problems with courage and understanding and humility so that you go ahead. Do not let karmic weeds increase on your path.

The fourth one is **treason**. Stay a friend with whomever you were a friend. Do not betray him. Do not engage yourself in treason. This is so important because the spiritual powers do not give you success, do not inspire you and protect you, if you are active in the work of betrayal and treason. If you stay away from treason, fear, and hatred, you already have the secrets of a successful life.

The fifth and sixth factors are **jealousy** and **revenge**. Jealousy and revenge are destructive emotions. They not only damage your body, but they also damage your brain. A jealous and revengeful businessman soon loses his head — then his business. "Jealous people destroy their own future because jealousy causes irrationality in their mind and leads them into destructive actions. There is an ancient proverb which says, 'Jealousy is like a strong viper which bites its container.' "[1]

---

1. *New Dimensions in Healing*, p. 205.

Chapter 5

Six Factors to Add for Success

To have success in your life, you must add

- courage
- daring
- cooperation
- service
- concentration
- meditation

First, develop **courage** because in business, in success, you always need courage. Do not talk about courage but try to exercise it. Some people say very courageous things to others, but they are not courageous. You are going to be courageous. What does being courageous mean? To be courageous means to open yourself and let your spirituality flow out. Instead of handicapping yourself, restricting yourself, and imprisoning yourself within your own failure images and obstacles, annihilate them with your fiery spirit. You are blocked by your past failures, past defeats, your hatred, malice, slander. Instead of being handicapped by such elements, release your spirituality and let your Real Self face the life.

Courage is a state of consciousness in which your own hindrances cannot block your progress. Courage steps on your vanity, ego, separatism, hatred, revenge, and treason and conquers them. That is courage. You are going to develop courage. You decide to exercise freedom in your expressions, in your service, in your relationships, without being the slave of the hindrances that you had in your nature.

Most of us are hindered. That is why we do not have courage. Our mother, our father, our priest has said, "You are stupid, you are good for nothing," and when we accepted such an image, we became "good for nothing." Courage means to destroy our past self-images and release ourself into new opportunities.

The second one is **daring**. People are confused between being daring and courageous. What is daring? Daring means to do those things that you think you cannot do. That is daring. "I cannot do it," is not the real you. That is *not* what you want. Instead, what you think you cannot do, do it. Dare to do it. You **will** do it.

You sit down and say, "I cannot do it." What is happening if you analyze the situation? You will see that there are many factors that are stopping you — past images, past failures, past defeats, negative announcements or statements about you, sometimes your own stupidities. They are blocking you, and there is no courage to break them and there is no daring to try again.

A girl came to me and said, "It is impossible for me to sit in front of the computer and type." Now she is typing one hundred twenty words per minute. How come? She dared! She was daring. Your challenge starts that moment when you think you cannot do something. Immediately awaken and say, *"Because I cannot do it, that is why I am going to do it."*

The third factor you are going to develop in your character is **cooperation**. Learn how to cooperate with people.

Here is something very important that you can do if you want to make cooperation a good tool for your success. Cooperate with people not for your own interest only, but cooperate mainly to make the other person more successful. *Your success is hidden in the success of the other person.*

The business world does not know this. Our modern businessmen do not think about this, but now a little light is shining here and there. Some of them are understanding that the best business is the one done in the interests of others because in the interests of others is the key to their own success.

As far back as we can imagine until today, everyone has wanted to be successful, healthy, and prosperous — for himself, his family, his religion, his nation. But that brought us to this stage of destruction. Now we are going to shift to just the opposite. "What business can I create so that millions of people will be happier and I will also be happy?"

You must see that the success of others is going to guarantee your ultimate success.

Suppose a great spiritual leader said, "I am spiritual. I am in the Father, and I have all these glories in heaven and on earth," but He did not come back here to make people really enlightened? He would not have any value. His success, His glory is measured by the success and the glory He gave or awakened and released in other people's lives. Because we are brainwashed by our tradition, religion, philosophy, and psychology, it is so difficult to think first of others. A business centered on ego leads to failure.

From now on search for, on your own, the rules and regulations and secrets of cooperation and how to cooperate.[1] See for yourself that cooperation is a prime factor for success. Imagine: Why are you healthy? ...Because your nervous system, your bones, your flesh, your eyes, your nose, your ears, all parts of your body cooperate with each other. Why are you sick and in the hospital? ...Because things within you are not cooperating. If you study this single example, you will be successful.

You see a wife sitting and crying; a man is hurting and cursing everyone in his business; children are not finding happiness at home, and there are millions of examples like this. Create cooperation by any means possible to you. Swallow your pride, your stupidity, your bigness or smallness and say, "Let us create cooperation," because in cooperation both sides are going to benefit.

The fourth factor is **service**. I hinted about this when I spoke about karma. You will never be successful, in its true meaning, if you do not *plant* for success. How can you plant for success? One day I went to visit the daughter of a friend who had fifty to sixty acres of land. My friend had died, and his daughter had inherited the land. She was waiting to see me. She said, "Come, come see my land." She had planted five thousand avocado trees, and they were growing so beautifully. She said, "Next year we

---

1. See *The Psychology of Cooperation and Group Consciousness* and *The Sense of Responsibility in Society.*

are going to have the best crop. Bring your car and fill it up." She knew that I love avocados.

Look what is happening. She is serving. She is planting for next year's crop. What are you planting to harvest next year in your life? That is what we are talking about. What are you planting? Are you planting avocado trees in your life now? The more you serve other people, the more your future will be glorious. And when you do not think about others, that is when you fail in your life.

> *The more you serve other people, the more your future will be glorious.*

There was a nation and its neighbor was contaminated with cholera. The government of the healthy nation thought, "That is our neighbor, but we do not care about it." What happened? All the viruses and germs came to their country and they were devastated also.

Now is the age of thinking about your neighbor more than yourself. How can we teach this to politicians? If you read the history of humanity, you will see that the law of success and victory worked on exactly the same lines. Those who cared about their neighbors, about other people and served them, were the people who survived.

The United States survived many depressions because we have rendered tremendous service to the world community in spite of all our mistakes. This is something that you are going to learn in your little life. How many people have you served?

When I was reading *Proverbs*, that wise man said, "Throw your bread on the river, and ages later you will find that bread." He was talking about karma. When you serve each other and do good to each other, you condition your future success; but if you are selfish, thinking only about yourself, that is the best way to fail in the future.

The fifth factor is to develop **concentration**. You must make your mental equipment successful by making your mind learn how to concentrate, how to analyze, how to see every side of a problem or an object. Then you must learn how to synthesize these into simpler parts so that you can see through them. This kind of action will exercise your mind and you will have a masterful piece of equipment in your head for your success, for solving your problems, and for serving other people.

It is very important that each of us think about expanding our consciousness, making our mental mechanism concentrate, making it see every side of a problem, how to analyze, how to synthesize. When we exercise all these, we will have a ready "car" to drive and to work for others in this life and especially in the next.

People are lost in their pleasures. Young girls, young boys, old men and women — sex, sex, drink, drink, pleasure, pleasure. Okay, have them, but you have lost time and your equipment is not ready. And, when you are going to "travel" in your next life, you will do crazy things because you did not repair your "car" now. Next time it will be more difficult to use it because the competition will be severe. For example, one hundred years ago if I wanted a typist, two or three among millions of people were able to type. There was no competition then. But now, when you put an ad in the paper for typists, hundreds of people will reply. Which one are you going to choose? How are they going to compete with each other? As ages go by you will have fewer chances to be successful *if in the past you did not prepare your vehicles for success.*

> *As ages go by you will have fewer chances to be successful if in the past you did not prepare your vehicles for success.*

Concentration prepares you for the sixth factor — **meditation**. Discipline your mind through concentration and meditation and use it for synthesis and analysis because the mind is the receiving unit of great ideas, visions, and revelations. Sometimes your logic in your business, in your field of service, is not enough. You need direct intuitive light, direct revelations, direct vision.

You need these also in your family life or friendships. Suddenly all your family members are angry with each other. Mother has a little vision and she says, "We are going on a picnic," and during the picnic the problems dissolve and everyone becomes happy. When the mind is organized in your own field of service, you receive great revelations, visions, solutions to your problems, new answers to your questions, and greater enlightenment.

You are going to work on your mind through *concentration.* When we say concentration, people think that we are referring to taking an object and concentrating the mind on it. Let us take a different approach. Look what concentration is. When you are washing your dishes left from a party, are you there, are you really washing, or are you thinking about other things, cursing, hating, being sorry that it is so late? Are your heart, mind, body, eyes, hands concentrated on what you are doing? If it is so, then that is a great success. If you are massaging a person and you are not there, it is not good. If you are shaking hands with somebody and you are not there, it is not good.

One day a lady told me, "When my husband hugs me, he is not there. When he kisses me, he is not there. He comes home and is not there. I do not know where he is." Well, this house is not going to be successful because he is *really* not there.

You type something and you are not there. Of course, there will be millions of mistakes and the boss will say, "I am sick of you." You are put in another position and you are not there. Where are you? Who knows? God save you. If you are not there, you do not have any concentration. You are going to be where you are. Your body, your attention, your concentration, your observation, your togetherness, all will be *there*.

When you give a speech or talk to someone, be clear and be there. This is how you will be really understood. But if you speak in a sophisticated language and float in the air and explain fantastic things, nobody will care about what you say because you are absent.

> *If you are doing a job, you must be there in the job, with the job. You must be fused with it.*

The other day I saw a boy shaking hands with a girl. He said, "I love you." She pushed him away and said, "What?" He was not there because he does not really love her. He was just making it up. Because he was not there, he was not sincere, he was not noble, he did not exist there. You go to your business, to the office, and find five girls sitting around. You say, "Hi, where are you?" They are at the beach; one is kissing her boyfriend; one is worrying about her mother. They are not there. The boss is going to discharge them.

The fifth factor then is to develop concentration. You must be there to be successful. If you are doing a job, you must be there in the job, with the job. You must be fused with it. You will turn into the job.

I have had this experience. Whenever I do something and I am absent from it, it does not give fruit. When I become the job itself, it is impossible that I am not successful.

You are going to be the job itself — not supervise it, no — you will be the job. I learned this when I was in the locomotive section of engineering in a railway station. I had six hundred people working for me. You should have seen what kind of people worked for me. Most of the time they were not there. Sometimes I would go and take their job and do it. Then they would see what I was doing and would get the courage and start doing things. You must be there in what you are doing. If you are not there, you develop absentmindedness, depression, and various nervous sicknesses. Try to be there in whatever you are doing.

And the sixth factor that brings success is meditation. "Meditation puts a man in contact with the Source, and eventually man is fused with the source of abundance within him. Meditation is a search for your Core, a search for what you are, where you are in your essence."[2]

---

2. *The Spring of Prosperity*, p. 15. For further information on meditation, see *The Science of Meditation*.

Question & Answer

Question: *Would you elaborate a little more on your earlier statement about outer cleavages and mental synthesis? Specifically, if I understand the principles which you are giving and want to apply them in my life but the other person does not respond mentally, is there still a way that I can heal those cleavages?*

Answer: First of all it is impossible that people will not respond when you are together. That is one of the greatest secrets. When you are really there, when you really mean what you say, when you really mean what you do, people, one hundred percent, will respond to you because people are the reflections of your state of consciousness.

People do not respond to you when you doubt yourself. When you ask people to help you but, in the meantime, you think that they are not going to help you, you have already failed. It is your state of consciousness that will mobilize other people. If other people are not helping you, are not cooperating with you, it means that you are not there.

Question: *What are the four directions of success?*

Answer: The four directions are: you, others, your environment, the environment of others. You can explain this in many, many ways. You do not only concentrate on what you are. You also consider what other people are doing. I learned this from driving on the freeway. Ten years ago, I only cared about how nice I was driving. Then I awakened. I said, "Hey, you can be a very good driver, but what about that driver who is drunk?" So I am now watching the other drivers, also, and figuring out what they are going to do the next minute. I am watching my car. I am watching the traffic. I am watching the freeway and what is going on. So it is not one-track-mindedness.

You are going to have an inclusive understanding about your situation and what is going on within you. For example, suppose you are buying a big piece of property at a time when the political situation is very bad or the financial situation is very bad or there are frustrations and different plans. You are going to put all these things into perspective and fit your plan accordingly. You need to expand your vision and find the right place and the right moment to start something or continue something.

Question: *How do we stop our fears?*

Answer: We stop our fears by facing our fears. For example, if I am afraid of something, I close my eyes and visualize the worst thing that can happen, and then I try to solve it in my mental plane, in the mental world. When I open my eyes, I do not have any fear because I am ready for the worst. Also, you must try to stop the sources of fear.

Question: *What if that fear is death?*

Answer: You can defeat the fear of death by gaining experiences of immortality, or continuity of consciousness. As long as you have no experience, such a fear remains in your heart.

Another way that you can minimize the fear of death is when you try with all your sincerity to serve people. Those who really serve gradually become souls, and when the soul is formed in them, they mentally reject the fear of death.

Question: *I have often had the fear of losing my children or my mother. How can I handle that?*

Answer: In your imagination and visualization lose your mother and let her go to heaven and take a new dress and come back. Why be afraid? The mother should not be afraid either. She is afraid because she is thinking that the sick body is so important. Of course if you can cure it, cure it; but if you cannot do it, do not be afraid. Think that she will be such a nice baby because she has a beautiful heart and has had a beautiful life. This kind of logic and visualization will help you discard that fear.

A friend of mine wrote, "I lost my father. I want to kill myself." "You stupid," I said, "in one day in my family Turks butchered eighty-seven doctors, lawyers, beautiful people. That is the life. Look what is happening? In the Middle East, Far East, Africa, here and there, they are butchering each other. Why to cry for one man who passed away? Let him pass away. That is his karma. Stand above it."

Fear is also pumped into your consciousness by your funeral homes.

> **Question:** *It is very difficult for a mother to separate herself from her children in that respect.*

Answer: That is why the mother fails. The mother fails because she identifies with the child and the child hates that. Allow the child to learn her lesson or his lesson. If he is dying, let him die. You do your best, but karma is unavoidable. Let it happen. It is the attachment that is our curse.

I love my five children, but then the time came when I said, "Go," and they did so well. Do not attach to them. If you ask your children, they will say, "The most obnoxious time I had with you was when you owned me, when you were attached to me." Allow them to experience life. Let them go and fly. Do your best to educate them, and then let them go.

> **Question:** *When you are not present in your dealings and in the functions of*

*your life but are absent in your think-
ing, it causes absentmindedness and
depression. What is actually happening?*

Answer: Absentmindedness and depression occur
when the real you is not present or existent in your
mind, in your thoughts, and in your emotions and
actions. When you let your mental, emotional, and
physical machines run the show, they wear out due
to a lack of energy coming from the real you. If you
do not open the faucet, the water will not irrigate the
field of your labor. If it is a worry, if it is a problem,
if it is a man, if it is a love, hatred, slander, whatever
it is, you are going to eliminate it so that you can focus
yourself on your job. Try again and again.

For example, I gave a package of match sticks to
a woman and said, "Throw them on the floor and then
assemble them head right, head left, head right, head
left *until you do not think about anything else except
about the sticks.*" This woman went for seven months
without finishing one box. Now she is doing the
whole box without thinking about anything else,
focused totally for one hour. Now she is so successful
in her dress selling business because when a customer
comes she says, "This dress is very good," and the
customer buys it because *somebody* is telling her. But
when the saleswoman is *not present* in her words and
showing the dress, the customer will not buy it because nobody is giving it to her; the saleswoman is
absent from her action.

Whenever we are present in our actions, feelings, and thoughts, they turn into energy sources and impress people.

> **Question:** *How does efficiency play a role in making us successful.*

Answer: Our whole intention is to make you an efficient person. Efficiency is a great aid to success.

Efficiency is a state of consciousness which causes the personality vehicles to be more creative with their action, emotion, and thought processes and produces higher quality effects in life.

Chapter 6

Rules for Success

There are many rules for success. Here are some very practical ones.

1. Try to solve your problems in a way that also considers the welfare of others.

2. Do things now that need to be done, and do not postpone them for tomorrow.

This is important advice, and most successful people proudly tell us that they never disobey this rule and that is why they have become successful.

3. Have a special place for everything and put everything in its right place.

Many successful people practice such a rule and they save their mind, energy, money, and time — which are important factors for overall success.

Your mental mechanism runs with less tension when you exercise these rules. If you put things in the proper place in your mind, you will have less problems in life. And if you do things that have to be done today, you save mental energy and prevent tension.

4. Do not spend all your energy, time, money, space all at once — reserve a little.

Exhaustion in any element of your life brings misfortune. No man can be successful in his job if he is wasting himself, his money, his time for his pleasures or is running day and night to be rich.

Every morning you must start your job fresh, energized, and with enthusiasm. No boss likes you if you are tired before you start your job. Successful people are full of energy, and they want energetic people in their business. It is energy that runs a business.

5. Learn the traditions, religions, customs, and beliefs of those people with whom you are going to work so that you know what kind of mentality you are working with. This is very important for mutual understanding and cooperation.

Know that you must *never* criticize their beliefs or customs or traditions. Your duty is to be the best co-worker in your present workplace. Belittling the beliefs or traditions of others creates hostility and distrust toward you, and you lose your position.

Of course, this does not mean that you are going to change your faith or traditions, but you are going to respect the faith or traditions of others. The best way to make people respect your beliefs is to respect their beliefs. You can work with people who have different faiths or beliefs only if you understand their faith and religion and hold an open-minded attitude. Actually, successful people never force their co-workers to believe the way they believe, and they expect their co-workers to do the same.

The best way to make people respect your beliefs is to respect their beliefs.

When some religious fanatics find a job, they immediately try to preach their religion to the boss and to co-workers. Some very successful people are not slaves of any religion, but have high moral and spiritual standards. They work to serve humanity. Do not be bothered about what people preach, but see how they live. Knowing the physical, psychological, and spiritual conditions of the areas in which you are going to work assists you in your success.

6. Pay attention to your health. You can be really successful and enjoy your success if you are paying attention to your physical health — digestion, assimilation, eyes, teeth, mouth, ears. All these things are important to make you successful. These rules are very basic, but people neglect them.

7. Learn how to sleep well because people who cannot sleep well will fail. They will eventually be defeated. You are going to see what is the best way to sleep in order to have a deep sleep and enough sleep. For example, if you are watching a stupid movie until three o'clock in the morning, you are stupid. If you are coming home from a party at eleven o'clock and making dinner for yourself, this is not good. You are going to find the reasons why you are not sleeping well and do exactly the things necessary for you to sleep well. For example, before going to sleep, you must get cleaned up: go to the bathroom, take a shower, clean everything, and then go to sleep in a nice place, without drinking and eating.[1]

8. You must exercise. Everyone of you must exercise. If you cannot do anything, just walk one or two miles daily or jump rope or swim or climb mountains. Every day you must have one hour of exercise. If you are not doing this, you may fail.

---

1. For information on sleep, please see *Other Worlds* and *New Dimensions in Healing*.

Volleyball, basketball, anything that you can do, do it — but exercise. Do not say that you are going to make money and be rich because when you get rich and you were not exercising, you will pay for your negligence with the money that you made. You are going to exercise. If you are heavy or not heavy, it does not matter. Whatever you are, start exercising.

9. People who breathe well are more successful people. I was reading in a newspaper that about forty years ago they started to examine the lives of successful people and they found something very interesting. *Successful people breathe deeply.*[2] Unsuccessful people breathe shallowly and take irregular little breaths. But successful people breathe nicely, filling their lungs with oxygen, hydrogen, and exhale nicely. It regulates their whole system, cleans the brain, and they are successful because they created successful conditions in their life. This is very easy to say but even our children, our grandmothers do not know that breathing is so important.

How are you going to do it? You start practicing deep breathing. Every day when you are walking a half mile or a quarter mile or fifty feet, start exhaling and empty out your lungs. Then with eight counts fill your lungs. Wait eight counts, holding the air in your lungs. Exhale it with eight counts, and hold your

---

2. See also *New Dimensions in Healing* for information on correct breathing.

lungs empty for eight counts. Then breathe again. This will make your lungs really beautiful and your face shining.

Whether you believe it or not, one of the causes of cancer originates from bad breathing. If you breathe well, the hydrogen and oxygen in your body will kill the germs and microbes and correct such conditions that create cancer. Those ladies who have difficulties in their breasts especially must know that they are not breathing well. Breathe well. Daily, practice good breathing for ten or fifteen minutes because health is success. If you do not have health and success, what else do you have?

10. Good food is next. You decide about your own food. There are many excellent books about nutrition. Read them and choose the foods that you should eat.

11. Along with good food you must think about your teeth. Not everyone takes care of his teeth. Many sicknesses originate from decaying teeth. If you go to work with your decaying and dirty teeth, maybe people will not even give you a job. But if you have beautiful teeth, people will want to hire you. Teeth are very important; do not neglect them. They are one of the factors for your success in the future because if you do not have good teeth, you have an ugly face and a rotten mouth. Make your teeth really good, which means morning and night brush them, clean

them, and do whatever is necessary to keep them healthy and beautiful.

12. Hair is also very important, especially for ladies but also for men. You must have a good looking hairdo because hair is an attraction device. When you go somewhere, your boyfriend, girlfriend, husband, wife looks at your hair. Take care of your hair and try to make it healthy. There are lots of methods you can use to make your hair healthier. Of course this brings auxiliary help for your success.

13. Cleanliness is another ticket to success. The other day a girl told me that a man smelled so bad that she did not want to work with him. Something in his body was unclean and smelly. Cleanliness is so essential. When you are hugging someone or when someone hugs you, you can smell whether they are clean or not. You are going to make yourself clean. I am not saying to put on a lot of perfume, but cleanliness is so important even if it is necessary to take two or three showers daily so that your body is clean, your hair is clean, your face is clean, your ears are clean. Sometimes in the ears you see dirty wax. How can you give such a person a responsible position? People do not pay attention to these small things and they fail. Also, an exaggerated use of perfume repels people.

14. Clean breath is next. Sometimes people come to me and say, "We would like to talk with

you." And I say, "Stay three feet away." They say, "What is the matter?" I say, "Nothing, I can see you better." The other day a woman came and she was right under my nose. I said, "Stay away a little." Her breath was awful! She asked, "What is the matter with you?" I said, "I am far sighted. I can see you better when you stay away a little."

You are going to kiss your girlfriend, boyfriend, wife, or husband, but there is an offensive smell. It is so important to clean your mouth and do something, whatever is necessary. Bad breath comes from the fermentation in your stomach, so you are going to take care of your stomach and digestion, and also care for your emotional states, and mental states because they all contribute to your breath. Your mouth must smell good.

15. A good walk is important. I was in a firm where they were hiring women and men. The man from the firm asked me how I would evaluate the women. I said, "Look at how they are walking." Two or three years later they told me they understood why the walk was so important.

Which girl are you hiring, the one who is walking like an elephant or a fox? If you pay attention you will understand how they are walking and what that walking signifies about their character.

Learn how to walk. I suggest that daily for two or three minutes you walk in front of a mirror very beautifully, rhythmically, harmoniously and do the best that you think you can do. Then watch how people walk. Watch how some people are walking and try to think which one would you hire if you wanted someone to work for you or be your friend. It does not matter whether you are heavy or lean. It is the tempo of your walking, the way you are moving. Walking expresses all your psychology.

16. Manners and a sense of responsibility are very important. For example, when I was in the British Royal Air Force, an officer and I were interviewing three girls for a secretarial position. The officer left a pin on their path as they entered our office. The first one looked at the pin and walked on to sit with us and talk. The second girl did not even see it. The third one saw it, picked it up and put it on the table, and then interviewed with us. We took that girl because she was observant and she had a sense of responsibility. That girl became the best secretary.

You must watch people's behavior: how they talk and what they talk about, how they walk, how they sit. Sometimes a girl comes to your office for a job and asks immediately whether you are married or not. This is not a smart way to interview. Or she starts to speak about her past. "I had five husbands and we were very rich, and I can type very well. What do you think of five husbands?"

Behavior should be noble. Watch your facial expressions, the tone of your voice, the movements of your hands, your walking, your dressing, your hair, your smiles. All these things affect your success.

17. Demonstrate firmness in your life. When you are relating to people, let them see firmness in your thinking, in your planning, in your decisions, in your goals. If I ask how many words you can type in one minute and you say, "I think sixty to two hundred," there is no firmness there. "I type one hundred-ten words per minute." Firmness. "Can you come to my office at eight o'clock sharp?" "Oh, I do not know but I will try." That is no good. You will say, "I can come." "Can you do this job?" "Yes, I can do it in one-half hour." You are going to be firm, concise, and correct in whatever answer you give. This is important also in your relationships, cooking, cleaning at home, everything. If you demonstrate firmness in your attitude, you will be appreciated far more than if you do not have any firmness in your character.

18. The next one is clothing. Try to dress well, in a way that is simple and fitting to the atmosphere. Bad choices in clothes may create rejection and tension in people. The way you dress must be appropriate to the job you are doing. Many people lose their job when they dress in a sloppy or even in an extravagant manner. Simplicity is recommended for acceptance.

Consider the occasion to determine what to wear, even what color to wear. Colors can be important when you are being interviewed for a job. If you are not dressed right, no matter how clever you are, they will not accept you. The color and the shape of your clothing have an effect on your future employer. These are outer aids for success, but they reflect your inner maturity and sensitivity.

One time when I was in a parking lot, I saw a girl who was dressed in such tight clothing that you could see everything on her body. If you are going someplace to get a job or see your boyfriend who does not like such kind of dressing, you must dress properly for the occasion. You are going to figure out how you are going to dress, in what color, in what shape, so that you create a pleasant atmosphere in your interview or relationships.

In all of your clothing, you are going to be economical, not outrageous. If you are fixing your hair, do not make it look like a movie star; it is too much for others to assimilate. Be modest in your dressing and makeup; otherwise, the boss will be leery of those who have diamonds hanging from their nose and ears! That is too much. You are going to be modest in your appearance.

19. Develop emotional stability. Many people in their life demonstrate emotions that are "anti-success." For example, whenever you are in a hot temper, demanding, commanding, angry, and jealous, you make others reject you. Emotions are so important to being successful. If you pay attention to these things, you will really be successful.

20. Do not live in fear. If you are always living in fear, no one will want to marry you or have you as

his friend or even hire you. Such a fearful person drives others crazy. If you have an employee or a partner who is always in fear, it is very difficult to work with him. If you are expressing continuous fear in your life, you are becoming a factor for rejection. People reject you and when they reject you, you are failing in life.

Fear prevents the help that comes from higher realms. Great Ones cannot send you inspirations and directions because of your fear which, like a massive cloud, surrounds you.

To destroy fear, face your enemies, whether inside or outside.

Question & Answer

Question: *What happens if you are firm but you are wrong?*

Answer: Firmness is related to being correct. If you are not correct, you are not stable, not firm. Firmness is based on correctness, on factuality, on reality, on truth, and even simplicity. If you appear firm but you are wrong, you send a subjective signal that you are unstable in your consciousness and people reject you.

Question: *What is the significance of these suggestions on higher planes? How do they help in our ultimate success?*

Answer: Nice dressing, nice teeth, nice health, nice breath, nice digestion, nice walking, nice behavior mean that you are a together person. If you are not a together person, you are not fit for a responsible job. That is what we are saying. These seem to be minor things but *they are signals of your character*, and if your character is not together, then you cannot fit into higher jobs or more responsible jobs.

For example, if you come to my office and say, "For fifteen minutes I was driving. I feel so tired. It was awful. The weather was so hot." What am I going to think about you? I will think, "This girl is weak. I am going to give her a big job, heavy work, heavy labor. If she is going to complain to me, I will not be satisfied with her labor." Already with your words you are demonstrating characteristics which do not fit a responsible position. You should say, "I drove four hours but I feel so energetic. Now, can I do something for you?" I will take that girl. When I say to an applicant, "What can I serve you?" and she says, "Oh, I feel really tired. I will take a little coffee," I will think she is hanging on me. I will feel she will excuse herself when she is tired. Wouldn't you like someone who is energetic to work for you?

I was once sitting in a restaurant. A couple was eating at the next table. The girl was very pretty; the boy was very handsome. The girl said, "You know, I feel so tired because you drove half an hour and I just hate driving. The boy said, "All right, what if you order this and this and this," and she began to eat everything like a pig. Then he asked, "Are you always like this?" "No," she said, "I am worse than that." I felt that the boy decided not to go out with her anymore. If a person is not noble, if she is hanging on him, if she is waiting there for everybody to serve her and she is so tired, so exhausted, so ignorant, so failed, so defeated, then why would he take on such a burden? Many of us do not think about such points.

You are going to demonstrate, not artificially but in actuality, that you are really somebody and you are going to be successful. A man came to me and said,

"I am opening a big business and I think that I am doing everything to make it beautiful, with everything neat and shining, but I know in my heart that I am not going to be successful." I said, "You stupid, why even start that business? The patterns of your consciousness are not right, are not pro-success, pro-victory; they are pro-defeat, pro-failure." When you are expressing such negativity, you cannot be successful in your life.

Your appearance, your dress, your hairdo reflect what you are inside. Also, your outer appearance changes your psychology. Dress well, and you will feel more confident. Dress sloppily, and you will feel insecure. Your inner and outer beauty must cooperate or reflect each other.

> **Question:** *If you had two people come to you for an interview and one of them had pretty hair, pretty teeth, dressed very well, presented herself really well, and really did not need the job and you had someone else come to you who was not as well off but who was loyal and hardworking, had children to support, and really needed and wanted that job, which one would you take?*

Answer: That is very easy. One is a show-off, and one is real. It is not your clothing that is going to make a big difference. It is proper dressing, the way that you dress. You do not need to dress in a two hundred dollar dress. You can buy material and dress yourself very beautifully, and that is more attractive than a show-off. An experienced boss will know immediately. If it is cosmetic, if it is plaster, he will immediately know that she or he does not fit the job. Of course, there are many, many tests to know people, but the most important thing that you are going to demonstrate is that you want to be successful, that you are ready to be successful, and you are ready to do anything noble to be successful. If that spirit is there, no matter how you dress, even if your hair is not too neat, it does not matter because it can be corrected if the spirit is there. *But, of course, it is better if the outer appearance reflects an inner maturity.*

I was reading a book about success. The author was teaching every kind of trick to force yourself in and take the job: how to deceive the boss, how to imitate and use various psychological techniques, even how to overthrow the boss and take over. Of course, such techniques may work, but they do not make you enjoy the fruits of your job. Instead, gradually they make you a miserable human being who works against his future success.

Anger, hate, jealousy, selfishness, self-interest, slander, revenge, malice, treason — these kinds of things destroy your success. Even if you are successful, even if you have inherited much money and a business, when you have such emotions, eventually you lose everything.

A gentleman was talking about three people who owned a business, and they were very smart people. They had forty people working for them. Now they only have four employees because they always criticized, belittled, and hated them. They were jealous of their employees. They were self-seeking people, self-important people. They tried to manipulate and exploit. Eventually their work went down and down. They lost their employees because they had these kinds of negative emotions in their hearts.

If you are going to be successful, you are going to shape whatever is involved in your physical, emotional, and mental life. Then you will become a magnet. Success will come to you, and you will enjoy it and make other people enjoy it.

If you have a co-worker, never try to capture him or her with sexually suggestive behavior. That leads to complications and eventual failure. Especially, do not do this with your boss. You will create many problems and may hurt the business. Come to the job with your efficiency. Let your efficiency talk instead of your body, instead of your sex, instead of your exaggerated jewels and diamonds. Try to gain attention by showing that you are a capable, efficient person. Let your efficiency talk.

Two young men went to a ranch looking for jobs. The boss asked these boys, "Do you know how to ride a horse?" The boy who really knew how to ride said, "Not too bad." The one who did not know said, "Oh yeah, I ride really well." The boss was sneaky and said, "Get on this horse and let me see how you ride." Immediately when the boy got on the horse, the horse threw him off. The boss said, "You are knocked down already. I will take this other boy," and that boy rode so beautifully.

Showing-off does not work. You are going to approach people with your efficiency, with your sincerity, with your good motive. That is what makes you successful.

Chapter 7

What to Develop for Success

Try always to develop *clear thinking* in your business and in your environment. What is clear thinking? Clear thinking is thinking that is *not* influenced by your hatred, fear, anger, jealousy, slander, and self-deceit. If these emotions are mixed into your mind, you will never think clearly because your emotions will think for you. You are not going to let your negative emotions think through you. You are going to think yourself. If you are free from your negative emotions, then you become a clear thinking person. A clear thinking person sees things as they are and tries to be himself. These are keys for success.

You are going to develop *reasoning*. What is reasoning? It is so simple. Reasoning is to wait one minute and think what will happen if you do this, if you talk that way, if you think this way. That is reasoning. If you hit someone, what will happen? That is reasoning. If you lie to someone, what may happen? That is reasoning.

> *Reasoning is to see the connection of the cause and the effect.*

Reasoning is to see the connection of the cause and the effect. For example, you are taking drugs. Okay, God save you. But you do not have reason and logic behind it. Why? ...Because you are not thinking about what that drug is going to do to you. Once you start thinking and seeing that this drug will cause you endless damage, you will stop it.

No matter at what level you are reasoning, it is good for you. Ask yourself, "If I become angry with my mother, what can happen?" It is reasoning. "If I am lazy, sleeping until eleven o'clock, is it all right?"

Reasoning is to watch your thoughts, your words, and your actions and think what they can produce in the future for you. That is reasoning. If you write a certain letter, how will the receiver feel? How is he going to react and what disturbances and problems are you creating with this letter? That is reasoning.

Develop your reasoning because reasoning is a great agent in your success, in your victory. If you do not have reasoning, you will not be successful.

Absence of stupidity is next. You lose many opportunities and defeat yourself through stupidity. *Stupidity is thinking, talking, and acting against your own interests.* Anything you are thinking that is against your future interests is stupid. Think how much stupidity you had in the past, doing things mentally, emotionally, physically that hurt you.

> *Inclusiveness means to relate even opposing factors and make them cooperate with each other.*

The next factor to develop is *inclusiveness.* You can be more successful in your life if you are mentally more inclusive. *Inclusiveness means to relate even opposing factors and make them cooperate with each other.* Nature does that.

Inclusiveness in your labor manifests as understanding people — their limits, their level of efficiency, their needs, their aspirations. In inclusiveness you think about your co-workers as your partners, and you deal with them accordingly. When your co-workers feel that you are including them in your business, they help you to be more successful. Inclusiveness creates cooperation in people and makes them serve your business better. Try to develop a measure of wise acceptance and inclusiveness.

Another factor that you are going to develop is *humility*. People really hate arrogant people, prideful people, show-off people. Such people advance a very short distance; then they fail. The more humble you are, the farther you can go, the more you will have to offer, and the more people will love you. When you are prideful, you are a sealed box. Nobody can increase anything in you because you think you already know!

I was reading about five very eminent business people's lives. They were very humble people. One man was a millionaire, and he had an old truck. One day he saw some lumber falling from another truck. He took it in his truck and went ten miles to give it back to the owners and they asked, "Who are you." He said, "I am just me." Later they found out he was a millionaire. His humility surprised them.

One of our great Presidents went to the forest and saw ten soldiers arguing with each other because they had a big log to move. The sergeant was saying, "Lift it and put it in the wagon." And the soldiers were saying, "It is very heavy." The sergeant was not even touching it. The President came up and took the log with the ten soldiers and together they put it on the wagon. Then the sergeant said, "I want to thank you. What is your name?" To the embarrassment of the sergeant he said, "Oh, I am the President of this country." That is humility. Be humble in your own activities, and you will be successful.

Try to *adapt your voice to the conditions* and the atmosphere of your job and work. If you pay attention, it will be very helpful for your advancement.

As much as possible, *talk only when it is necessary*. That will develop in you the power of discrimination, the power of listening, the power of observation. These are three additional things that can make your life more successful.

Sometimes I used to listen to my employees when they were talking about business on the telephone. They spoke about things that were not necessary at all. Answer questions in a concise and clear way and do not say things or tell stories that are not related to business.

Develop carefulness in speech so as not to talk more than is needed. That is a very important factor and the most difficult to learn. Until I learned how to talk on the telephone, I made millions of mistakes. In all your relationships you are going to think first how to speak because too much speech that is not fitting to the conditions saps your energy, electricity, and magnetism and creates confusion or rejection in others, and that hurts your success.

Before you talk, before you relate to people, *see in what condition they are living*, in what situation they are living, and what is their background. A person's background is so important.

In the book *Woman, Torch of the Future* I wrote some shocking statements. A woman psychiatrist did not like what she read in that book and wrote me a very nasty letter. One day I heard that she was coming to my city to give a seminar. I said, "I wish I could see her and talk with her." Before I had a chance, she called me. She said, "I need three hundred copies of that nasty book you wrote." I said to myself, "Control yourself." Then I said to the lady, "I am so happy that you are ordering that book. We will dispatch them immediately." She said, "At first I did not like that book, but after I thought and meditated, I found that it is one of the best books written on the subject." She sold three hundred copies at her seminar and ordered another two hundred.

She had been concerned about the paragraph where I said, "Before you become engaged to a boyfriend or girlfriend, check the background of the parents, grandparents, to see what disease they died from, etc." Now science is proving that your genes, viruses, and inheritances can infect you even four generations later. In the future when you start creating new ties, new communications, new relationships, always go to the history of that man, of that woman, father, mother, grandmother, grandfather. That will give you more success because you will be less involved with unexpected problems.

Be very slow in expressing your opinions and your interpretations. For example, you are sitting with a group of people and every minute you are expressing your opinions and interpretations of things. Very soon people will be looking at you and thinking what an egg-headed person you are. You can create more respect with your silence, and such respect allows you to be more successful. Be economical in expressing your opinions and interpretations of things. First know what they may think, what they may feel, what they may accept, what they may reject. Then maybe after ten meetings, you can express one percent of your interpretation so that they do not react against you, feel threatened, or think you are a nut.

> *You can create more respect with your silence, and such respect allows you to be more successful.*

Concentrate, learn, and make yourself ready for everything in which you are engaged. For example, if you are a typist, study typing, study the computer, study your fingers, study how to be grammatically correct. In any field, start promoting yourself by learning and making yourself ready for new challenges. In any job that you are handling, do not take for granted that you know everything. Try to know more about that field and try to make yourself more efficient to meet new and unexpected challenges in that field.

I was in the Middle East where I was working as a steam engineer. One day the head engineer asked, "Do you want to take a ride with me? We will be gone for seven hours. There is a horse race at the other end that we can watch for two or three hours."

I love horses so I said, "Let's go."

> *...start promoting yourself by learning and making yourself ready for new challenges.*

We started out in the locomotive, but four or five miles ahead we saw that there was a huge truck stopped on the tracks. I wondered what my boss was going to do. I immediately started pulling the horn and he said, "Leave it alone, leave it. You will see what will happen." He did not lose his calmness.

We were going ninety miles per hour, and then he made it one hundred and twenty miles per hour in two or three miles. He opened all the steam, all the electricity. We were going like a knife. We cut the truck in half and nothing happened to our train. We had about five hundred passengers on board.

I asked, "How did you think to do that in two or three seconds?"

"Well," he said, "I did not think about it now, but I always have a habit to think about what I would do if something like that happened, and if it happens I am ready to act as I thought."

Later I learned in physics that if you are a certain weight and are going at a certain speed, then you have power to cut even a cement wall. Increase your speed, your velocity, and you will be safe.

You must think about how you are going to face new challenges and answer new problems if they suddenly pop up. That is how you must make yourself ready in your career. In whatever you are doing, be the professor of it.

The next item is that in all your relationships, especially in your labor and business, *keep your joy.* Be joyful because joy is one of the keys to great success. If you are getting engaged, do it with joy. If you are getting married, do it with joy. If you are starting a business, do it with joy. If you are forming a family, keep joy in the family. If you want to be healthy, be more joyful. If you are building a group, take those people who are joyful.

> *True joy has such a deep solemnity that it attracts people to you.*

Do not take depressed people because they will ruin your job or your group. Or, make them joyful and then take them. Joyfulness is very important in all your relationships. Even if you are the boss and ten people are working with you, demonstrate joy because they will love you. Everybody is thirsty, hungry for joy. Give them joy and they will give you success. True joy has such a deep solemnity that it attracts people to you.

I know many girls and many boys who make their bosses crazy by hanging on them with their depression, complaints, and slander. Eventually the boss says, "I am sick of you. You are fired."

> *...know that the life you have now is nothing else but the life that you wanted to have.*

The next thing is *do not complain.* If necessary directly meet the one who is making you complain and talk over the problem. Complaints sap your electromagnetic energy. Complaints turn other people negative toward you. Even people who love you become negative if you start complaining. Do not complain about anything. If you have problems, sit down and talk. Say, "This is happening. Can we improve it scientifically, philosophically, psychologically? Let's improve it." But if you are complaining, you are harming yourself seriously.

I was advising a young woman who got married. She used to hang on her husband and complain. Immediately when he came home she would say, "The neighbors were too loud. The weather is so bad. I feel tired. The cat did this. The dog did that. I am sick of life." One day the man said, "I am sick of you."

Do not complain. Especially if you are an employee, God save you! Complaining is the worst thing and the best way to make your friends become your enemies. Do not complain to your father, your mother, your children. Complaining destroys the future possibilities of your success.

Do not pity yourself. Sometimes you must pay attention, really think about, and know that the life you have now is nothing else but the life that you wanted to have. In the past you worked hard to have such a life. Why complain if you have the life that you wanted to have? People condemn God, karma, earth, heaven, angels, and even Satan and say, "Why are we in this condition?" They are blind and they do not know that they wanted to have exactly the life that they have. Nature gave them the exact thing that they wanted. If you want to change your life, start changing it now.

Do not pity other people. Some people pity those who are not successful. If someone is not successful, that is what he wanted. When failing, one must tell himself, "You did this and this and this. These are the factors that led you into failure so, really, you worked for your failure."

I was saying to a girl, "You know, you slander, slander. According to you, nobody remained in the world who is any good. You make everybody bad. Do you think that you are the only flower on this earth?"

"Yes," she said. She is a great failure now because she thinks that she is somebody and everybody else is a cabbage. Such a philosophy leads you to failure.

Never gossip about your friends and co-workers and employees. **Never.** That is a very bad thing that people do. There was a girl who used to work years ago with me. I told her not to gossip about others. Believe me, up to now she has changed jobs twenty-two times. In every job she is thrown out because of the same defect of character. She gossips and she cannot get rid of this behavior.

Why are you gossiping with your co-workers? Everyone is what he is. Just shut your mouth and get along with them. She gossips about employees to employees; she gossips about her boss to employees; she gossips about the girls to the boss, and everyone goes crazy. You do not need these kinds of things in your life because they lead you into failure. It is not your business if she left her husband, boyfriend, girlfriend, that she was late. Mind your own business.

I knew a man in the Middle East. He was so cute. People would come and tell him, "Do you know what happened in the world?" He would say, "That is God's business. I do not want to hear." No matter how they gossiped and slandered, he would put himself out of involvement. They used to ask him, "Why did you do this or that?" He would answer, "It is my business." They used to tell him, "Nancy left her husband." He would answer, "That is her business."

He was very much respected and was a successful man in that town. He was, in the meantime, a very cooperative and progressive person.

Do not involve yourself with the trash of others by gossiping and slandering them. Somebody wrote me from Europe and said, "A man came and said such bad things about my brother that now I do not want to see his face."

You said bad things about someone, and you lost two friends. Instead, protect your co-workers, your friends, your relatives, and speak about something that is good in them. That opens success for you. Even if they have ninety-nine bad things, find one good thing and talk about that. That will lead you to success. You want to be successful, right? This is the science. You cannot improve people by hurting their feelings.

On the other hand, some people praise you to your friends to get their help, and then they slander you when they get what they want. Even in such cases try not to become involved.

If people come and complain to you, just listen indifferently and tell the complainer or gossiper that you do not want to be involved in it. When people come and gossip to you about others, listen very indifferently, even do not smile because they will say that you agreed. Do not say one word. Just listen. Say, "I do not want to be involved." Take yourself out of it. This will bring you success.

Once when I went to attend an educational organization, three boys came and caught me immediately. They said, "You have two or three days vacation. After that you will be busy with the classes. So we want to take you to the mountains, to the rivers, everywhere. We will show you the countryside."

With the permission of the boss we went, and what they began saying was this, "You know, the boss is the most stupid man. You do not know yet." I was new there, and I did not know why they were talking that way. They said, "We are a gang and you will be with us." But they did not tell me that it was all fabricated to test me. I said, "I did not come here to listen to this trash. You are taking me to the river. Let's swim. Let's enjoy life and go back. Ten days later the boss called me. He said, "Are you with the gang?"

I said, "What gang?"

"Didn't three boys take you and say I was a very bad man?"

I asked, "What are you talking about?"

He said, "From now on you will be with us."

I did not insult the three boys who were intentionally asked by the boss to test me, and I did not talk against the boss nor against the boys. Do not involve yourself in such tricks. Stay above them.

In your business *do exactly what you are told to do*. If you want to change anything, ask the advice or permission of your superior. That is a very delicate matter, and I have seen in many businesses how people failed when they did things that they were not told to do.

One day we were working in a house and the boss said, "Do not open that window," but one of the workers opened that window and three rattlesnakes came in. The boss came and saw the rattlesnakes and asked, "Who opened the window? There was a nest there." He made the man quit his job. "Go away," he said. "You are not going to work here because you did not obey my command."

Do exactly what your boss wants you to do. If you want to change something, go and discuss it with him so that you are really sure before you decide that he is giving a command that is nonsense. Ask him. Maybe there is a reason. That is very important for business.

If you have a boss that you do not agree with or he tells you things that you do not think are right but you do not want to go against the boss, you have two choices. You can tell the boss, "I feel that you are wrong, but I respect you. I am going to leave you." Or you can say, "I feel that you are wrong but I respect you, so I am going to stay here and continue working." There are no other ways. You are going to be very sincere and tell him that he is wrong in your opinion because of one, two, three, four, five, six things. If he does not admit his mistake, then you are going to choose either to continue or to leave the job. That is it.

You should not fight with the boss. The boss is the boss, but you can enlighten him if he is mistaken. Some bosses, even if they are mistaken and you have told them they are mistaken and they know that they are mistaken, continuously insist that they are not mistaken in order to save face. So you are going to give them an opportunity to save face.

I was once working in a machine shop. The boss was installing a part the wrong way. He was really a magnificent mechanic, but at that particular time I do not know what the matter was. I was tempted to say, "This is wrong; put it this way, that way," but I caught myself and shut my mouth. I thought, "I am not going to tell him anything."

Then he said to me, "What do you think. How does the machine look?"

I said, "Do you want me to check over what you did?"

"Well, whatever you want to do. Just check everything to make sure everything is in the right place." And he went away to his office.

So I came to him and said, "I learned from the books that this part must be put in differently. I know that my former teacher told me to put it in another way, but you did it differently. What about if you check it once more?"

He came and examined the parts and said, "That is wrong. Did you change it? I didn't put it like that; you changed it."

"Oh," I said, "maybe I did." Three weeks later he called me to his office and said, "Ten dollars extra will be added to your salary because you were very noble and did not humiliate me in front of others. I was wrong."

There are techniques that you can use in some difficult situations. You see, your whole intention will be to be successful. It is an art. Deal with people in a way that your behavior helps you to be successful.

Life helps everyone to be successful, if one does not follow the path of self-defeat.

If you have no prosperity, do not blame others or the Most High. Search for causes within you and in your relationships. Look for your motive.

If you have no prosperity, do not blame others or the Most High....Look for your motive.

Chapter 8

Success for the Future

You can be successful in your life when you help other people be successful. This is an advice or a rule for the future of humanity. All businesses and politics are going to go toward this. Unless you go toward this rule, you are going to destroy yourself and the world. You can be successful as an individual, as a family, as a business, as a corporation when you work for the success of others and make them successful. The more you make them successful, the more beautiful you are.

There was a man in a silly story that I read. This man used to sell meat to a little village and because the meat was not selling quickly and they did not have refrigeration, he sold rotten meat and made money from all the villagers. But the villagers started dying, and he went bankrupt. *You are successful because of your customers, because of how you help others. The happier you make your customers and other people, the more successful you will be.*

Second, whenever you are opening a business or starting any relationship or any form of endeavor that you are going to create in your life, first sit down and think how you can organize that business or that corporation or that work or that relationship in such a way that it helps others, not only you. The real foundation of your organization must be for the good of the people, even if it is necessary for you to forget all your interests in the interests of the others. That will bring you huge amounts of success, but unfortunately we have built our consciousness in just the opposite way. We are going to shift our consciousness and change it.

The next one is to give your money, advice, and encouragement to make people successful. Put in your mind that at least once a year you will make someone, some group successful. Just put it in your mind. This year you must vow to do those things that make people successful, more educated, more beautiful, healthier. When you think about the success and prosperity of others, you are already conditioning your future success and prosperity.

I was traveling from New York to Los Angeles and a man asked me, "What are you going to do in California?"

I said, "I am going to write books."

"Oh," he said, "you do not even know English. You cannot write books."

I said, "My English is not so good, but I have great ideas. Eventually ideas will help build my language and maybe I will be able to talk better than I do now, but I am going to write books."

"Books do not bring money to you," he insisted.

I said, "I am not writing books to bring money. I am writing to tell people something that I feel will benefit them."

He said, "That is stupid!"

Years passed and I became really successful. How was it that I became successful? ...Because I did not do it to make money. I did it to help people. That is what I want to convey to you. When you are opening a store, a stationery store, a health food store, even a restaurant, your first thought will be, "I want lots of people to come and benefit from my labor." The restaurants that really think about the health of people are the most successful restaurants. Those people who want to make only money cut corners and eventually lose their whole business.

The first thing you must consider is, "What can I do for people to be successful?" There was a man who came to a city and saw that in the city there was no water, so he started to dig a well. He dug a well and very pure water came and the villagers were thrilled, "Wow, we have water now." He said, "Here drink it," and he was not asking one penny. These people built a palace for him and gave him everything to be the happiest man because he never thought about digging a well to make money for himself. He wanted to dig the well to quench the thirst of the people.

Another story I read was about a man who went to a village in the wilderness. They did not have vegetables at all. He said, "How come these people are not eating well? They need vegetables." So he created a lot of compost and he mixed this and that, and built hot houses for vegetables, and many people came to help him. Eventually that little village became a source of vegetables for a big city and all the people there became very wealthy.

"What can I do for people to be successful?"

Look what one man did! But our whole intention, in whatever we do, has been first to think of what is going to come to us. That is why, even if wealth comes to us, we do not enjoy it because we are approaching success from the negative side of the business rules, regulations, and laws.

Do not discuss your personal life, your failures, your defeats with your co-workers or your boss. Be professional and impersonal. That brings great success to you. Immediately when the boss smiles at you,

you reveal everything that you did in the past. "I had five hundred boyfriends." Really? "I was sick with that sickness. I divorced this way and that way." What are you doing? You are revealing and exposing your obnoxiousness, your past faults, and you are not going to build a good image in the mind of your boss or leader. He is not asking you about your past obnoxiousness. Close your mouth and answer his professional questions. That is so important for your success.

Do not talk about your past greatness, victories, or successes. Demonstrate now that you can do the best job, professionally, and await recognition. For example, you want a secretary and you can pay six dollars per hour. Okay, this secretary comes and says, "Good morning," and she is lovely. She can type really professionally. But she opens her mouth and says, "You know, in the past, I used to make twenty-five dollars per hour and I had a Mercedes and I lived in a great house." The boss will become very wary. "I cannot hire this person because if I give her six dollars now, she will be very uncomfortable and will eventually leave. Now I do not want this girl." Then the boss says, "Okay, I will think about you." And the next girl comes and the boss asks, "How much are you asking for this position?" She says, "I would like four dollars per hour." "Okay, I will hire you and give you six." The boss will choose the second one, provided she meets the needs, because the first one boasted so much that it made the boss wary of her. This is very practical advice.

A student wrote to me. "I have written many, many books. I have graduated from five schools, completed many lessons and classes, and I want now to take your correspondence courses." I said, "I do not have anything to offer you because you already know everything." That was a defect in his character, boasting about himself and telling me that he had done many things in the past. Suppose a man came and said, "You must respect me." "Why?" "...Because in the past we had five thousand cattle on millions of acres." But you will think, "Why respect him if he is so boastful of his past?" You want to see what he has now and what he can do now!

Be indifferent toward those who praise you or flatter you or blame you. These are often signals of bad intention. If people praise you, be very careful. If they scold you, be very careful because maybe it is a test to reveal what you are. Be indifferent toward the praise and the blame and take them professionally. If they are saying that you are just wonderful because you can type a hundred pages in one hour, you know that is flattery. You know it. If they say that you are the worst human being, do not accept it because you are not. Stay in your clear thinking, demonstrating indifference toward praise and blame.

Be punctual in office hours or any work that you are doing. Many successful people are not only punctual, but are always a little bit early to prepare their work.

If you are working for a boss, once a month have an interview with him and ask if you need additional training, or improvement in your character and relationships.

If you are the boss, once a month have a meeting with your employees and ask them if they have new ideas for improvement. You can use the occasion to give new guidance.

Do not work in places that are engaged in selling drugs, pornographic literature, alcohol, or are devoted to illegal activities, exploitation, and separatism against the human race or your country. Never work as an employee in those places where the boss is dishonest, sectarian, separative, and manipulative.

Success not only needs physical, emotional, and mental preparations but also something beyond it. It needs faith. There are many definitions of faith.

> *...every labor, in order to bring success, must be dedicated to the Most High and done for the service of humanity.*

Faith is the process of demanding from the Universe that which you want and an intuitive knowledge that your demand will be met. Without such a faith there will be no lasting success. Do not start any work without faith.

There is another factor which is very important for your success. Every work and every labor, in order to bring success, must be dedicated to the Most High and done for the service of humanity. Remember that not only does the environment affect your striving, but through your striving you also influence your environment. The powers that you must exercise are

- The power not to be influenced by the negative factors of your environment

- The power to annihilate the negative factors in your environment and introduce pro-survival factors

You are equal to the creative influences that you exercise on your environment. Your spiritual influence upon people decides what you are.

For example, if you have unity and integrity within yourself, you create groups that are united and integrated. You create group consciousness in people.

Your influence can be recognized as destructive or constructive. Ego, vanity, superiority, and inferiority concepts must be destroyed. But group consciousness, humility, cooperation, and recognition of the Inner Divinity must be cultivated and developed.

Question & Answer

Question: *If you are doing things for other people, then how are you going to pay your own rent if you are not getting paid?*

Answer: What you should be concerned with is your motivation. We are talking about your motivation. For example, if you are a doctor and you have ten patients that you are treating but your prime interest is in how much money you are going to make, that is the wrong approach. But if your real intention is to help these people and forget yourself, the money will come — plus you will feel great.

Success is not dependent on physical things. It comes from subjective realms. Your motivation must be right, and, if you start that way, you will see how rich you will be and how you will be able to enjoy it.

The principle spirit of creating a business is "How can I help people?" Business is the expression of your will-to-help people, and through helping people you help yourself to continue to help others.

How can you reap if you do not sow? This seems very simple. Some Great Ones were asked, "Why are these people so rich and able to enjoy their lives so beautifully?" They said, "Because in the past they helped so many people."

A stranger was sitting on a rock by a big river and suddenly he fell into it, but by chance two men came and saved his life. He said, "I am so grateful that you saved my life, but I wonder how you came to be here?" Life arranged to save him because in the past he used his life to help people.

Whatever you sow, you are going to reap. Do not forget that. If you are killing, they will kill you; if you are robbing, they will rob you; if you are slandering, they will slander you; and this vicious circle will go forever and forever, making you more and more miserable. **Success is the ability to come out of this vicious circle.**

> **Question:** *Christ said, "Seek first the kingdom of heaven, and everything else will come to you." Is this what He was talking about?*

Answer: Yes, exactly. The motivation is the Kingdom. The Kingdom of God is within you. If your inner world has right direction, right principles, everything will come to you. You do not even need to run after things. Success will come to you as the result of your spiritual orientation, integrity, beauty, readiness, and magnetism.

Let us say that a great executive comes here and wants to hire one of you for a secretary. Who will be his secretary? The one who is the most ready physically, emotionally, mentally, and spiritually will be his secretary. Why? ...Because the secretary had prepared himself for success.

The world is a big computer and the computer is searching for the best people who can fit into certain duties and responsibilities, and life arranges for you to come to the right place to work. The only thing that you are going to do is demonstrate to the life that you *are ready* and that you are ready to work now. Whenever you are ready, your job is ready. **If you do not have a job, it means that you are not ready for the job you have in your mind.** You are going to make yourself ready.

> **Question:** *How can you get paid what you want when you are going for a job unless you ask for what you want? From my experience, if you ask for under what you want, they are going to give you under what you want.*

Answer: I did not say you should be underpaid. Ask yourself, "What is the job I have to do?" You know what the job is, and you know whether you are ready for it or not. If you go to the boss and say, "I have only two years experience as a building engineer, but I am ready to learn and promote myself. If you can use me, I am ready." You are very clear, very simple, very honest, but if you say, "I have worked fifty years" and you are twenty-five years old, he will say you are crazy. Be factual so that you attract his attention and love and appreciation. Even if you have faults and if he asks about them, tell him. "Do you smoke?" "Yes sir, I smoke but I think that I must stop." Well, you are honest. He would rather take you because you are honest than take another person who lies.

Be always factual and clear. That is why you must have clear thinking. Do not pretend, do not imitate, and do not fabricate. Be yourself. When you are five minutes late say, "I am sorry. I should have been here at eight o'clock, but there was an accident. I am very sorry to take your time, but if it is an offense being late I understand." It is clear, finished. Many people fabricate, and the boss knows or your wife knows or your sister knows that you are fabricating. When you fabricate you lose the possibility of your future success.

> **Question:** *If you really have a resistance in some area of your life to success, how do you know if you are fighting against karma or just being stupid?*

Answer: It does not matter. Karma is also an obstacle and a hindrance. You are not going to say: "Because I have karma, I am going to stay as I am." You are going to fight against your karma, raising yourself above the karma.

How can you do this? For example, let us say you are a builder. Build something and watch it and say,

"This is a very good building, but if I did this, this, and this, it would be a better building." You can develop a little more advanced observation within you so that you do better than before. If everyday you do a little better, eventually the karma that is stopping you from doing better will assist you.

Maybe you learned from ancient Greek history about the man who had something wrong with his mouth and he could not speak well. He suffered and tried to discover what to do. So he went to the seashore and started to put little pebbles in his mouth and then tried to speak. Eventually he became a better speaker, and then he became the greatest orator in Greece.

> **Question:** *A young tennis star beat another tennis pro. When they asked her how she did it, she said that her coach told her just before she went on the court, "Every ball you hit you are going to know how to handle and you will win." Now what key did he give her?*

Answer: He opened in her the spark of readiness. Sometimes you need encouragement to use your readiness. I have noticed this in my experiences. I learned to play the Hungarian Rhapsody on my violin, but at home I drove my sister, my father, and my mother crazy while practicing. When the time came for my recital, my legs were shaking. I was ready, but I was not ready. My Teacher came and hit me hard on the back and said, "Look in my eyes. You are ready; you can do it." I awakened. He took all that burden away, and I played very well. You sometimes need a good shock to awaken your readiness, but if you are not ready and your boss is saying you are ready, he is hypnotizing you. You must be ready to be ready.

Neither praise others, nor flatter them. Express joy in their success, and if they fail and ask you, tell them, "Seek for the causes on your own."

Question: *Is it a sin to have money or wealth through your labor?*

Answer: Some people think that it is a shame to have money, to have position, to have abundance. It is really a shame if your money is accumulated by robbing people, by hurting their future through various ways of manipulation. But if your money is the effect of your service for humanity, if your abundance is the gift of life because of your right motives in business, and if your position is in a field of helping people to help themselves, then your money and wealth and position are blessings to the world.

Chapter 9

Exercise

Here is a noble exercise which you can do. Every day tune yourself with the creative forces of Nature by doing the following:

1. Relax yourself and feel that all your essence is fusing with a yellow-blue light in the Universe, the creative force in Cosmos.

2. Say,

> *"May the warriors of the Lord shield me with Their fire so that evil and its agents are not able to touch me. Thank you, Lord."*

3. Visualize victory and success in serving humanity.

4. Then sit a few minutes in joy.

Chapter 10

Harmful Methods to Achieve Success

Every success achieved by methods that are harmful to another leads you to a personal "hell," methods such as:

— liquor sales

— drug sales

— prostitution

— killing animals

— manipulating old and sick people

Every serious pursuit for self-interest or separative interests brings pain and suffering.

Every success at the expense of others leads people away from the light of God to a future "hell."

Every success achieved by wrong means, such as cheating, or manipulating, creates a heavy tail of karma behind you.

These successes are cold paths leading to your future misery.

Chapter 11

❖

Success Tips

- Be joyful.

- Do not give up.

- Be optimistic.

- Know that God *is for success and victory*.

- The highest success is self-actualization.

- Speak slowly.

- Be sure to know what you are talking about.

- Make your voice pleasant, joyful, energetic.

- Always have a pleasant look on your face.

- Be content.

- Do not be greedy.

- Do not be aggressive.

- Do not have an "all for me" attitude.

Health, knowledge, appearance, and a sense of timing are very useful tools for your success.

Emotional stability is very important to help you obtain and enjoy success.

The following are diamonds on your path:

— Joyfulness

— Positiveness

— Gracefulness

— Respectfulness

— Gratefulness

The following is a list of mental assistants needed for success:

— Clear thinking

— Reason

— Logic

— Absence of stupidity

— Tolerance

— Inclusiveness

— Humility

— Absence of vanity, ego, and greed

Never argue with your boss or superior. Think things over carefully; then present your opinion in a calm and logical manner. Do not argue with your co-workers. Follow the instructions of your superior, and if you have reasons to present your opinion, do it, but follow his instructions if he insists.

You may have various opinions from your co-workers about the instructions of your boss, but your duty is to follow the boss if he is not violating your rights, or if he is not leading you to illegal paths.

Changing your goal often is like changing the location of your tree. It will eventually dry up.

Put all your heart, mind, and action into the work given to you. Do not constantly change your jobs, your career, your goals.

Changing your goal often is like changing the location of your tree. It will eventually dry up.

Chapter 12

Self-Importance

Every human being must feel important. One cannot respect himself and others if he does not realize that he and others are important.

When a person thinks he is important, he respects himself — which means he takes care of his physical body, his emotional relationships, his mental persuasions, and tries to become a useful member of the community.

But self-importance sometimes becomes inflamed by ego and vanity and turns into a sickness the moment a person begins to think that others are not as important as he is. When the ego is inflamed, the person changes his character and thinks he is the only important person. This leads to failure on all levels.

Such an illusion manifests as follows:

— "I am superior."

— "I know everything."

— "I can do everything."

— "Others are cabbages."

— "Everyone around me must serve me."

— "The Universe exists for me."

This is how the ego inflames and obsesses our consciousness. From that moment on there is nothing that we can give to humanity except problems and headaches. All our work and relationships become selfish, self-seeking, and egocentric. This creates a psychic wall around our Core and prevents the radiation of the sacrificial rays concentrated in our Core because we become so important in our eyes that everything we want is for us.

The psychology of service is just the opposite. Service is to give, to sacrifice, to radiate out, to expand the Divinity found within us. Success is based on the pure concept of service. One cannot be *successful*, in its real sense, if he is not engaged in a life of service.

Actually, service and success eventually fuse in each other and a person realizes that his *success* is his service and his service is his success. The more a person thinks about serving others, the more he will be successful; and gradually he will see that there is a *greatness* in him, and he will try to actualize that greatness in others through his service and success.

Service suffers when it does not have a spiritual vision. Spiritual vision is obtained through six steps:

— Meditation

— Creativity

— Intention

— Nobility

— Honesty

— Trustworthiness

The ultimate success of a person is much deeper than he can imagine. No success is eternal and everlasting except the success of

- Self-mastery

- Self-actualization

- Discovering your True Self

- Living in the glory of that Self

Those people who deepen their wisdom and experience in life suddenly realize that all their work to achieve success is a means for self-discovery and self-mastery. Such a realization is a great enlightenment for a person. From that moment of realization, all that a person does to achieve success will be considered a means to achieve Self-mastery.

The ultimate success for a human being is the discovery of his Inner Divinity and the actualization of his Inner Divinity.

Once a person has such a realization, he will handle all his mundane labor more successfully and with deeper co-measurement. He will be more successful from the viewpoint of the world, and more successful from the viewpoint of spiritual values. Thus, each of his worldly successes will be an expression of his spiritual success.

People have an idea that the Great Masters achieved mastery only in seclusion. This is not true. We are told that almost all of Them were great executives in Their many incarnations. They suffered and struggled like us, and eventually entered the path of mastery.

The ultimate success for a human being is the discovery of his Inner Divinity and the actualization of his Inner Divinity.

All else will be considered a failure if it is not used as steps leading to that Supreme Goal.[1]

---

1. Note: We suggest that with this book you also study *The Spring of Prosperity*, written by the same author, which will bring a deeper insight into your life of the true meaning of prosperity.

Bibliographic References

Saraydarian, Torkom. Sedona, AZ: Aquarian Educational Group.
The Science of Meditation, 1981.
The Spring of Prosperity, 1982.

Saraydarian, Torkom. West Hills, CA: T.S.G. Publishing Foundation, Inc.
The Ageless Wisdom, 1990.
The Flame of the Heart, 1991.
New Dimensions in Healing, 1992.
Other Worlds, 1990.
The Psychology of Cooperation and Group Consciousness, 1989.
The Purpose of Life, 1991.
The Sense of Responsibility in Society, 1989.

Index

About the Author

This is Torkom Saraydarian's latest published book in the Vision Series. Many more will be released very soon. His vocal and instrumental compositions number in the hundreds and are being released.

The author's books have been used all over the world as sources of guidance and inspiration for true New Age living based on the teachings of the Ageless Wisdom. Some of the books have been translated into other languages, including German, Dutch, Danish, Portuguese, French, Spanish, Italian, Greek, Yugoslavian, and Swedish. He holds lectures and seminars in the United States as well as in other parts of the world.

Torkom Saraydarian's entire life has been a zealous effort to help people live healthy, joyous, and successful lives. He has spread this message of love and true vision tirelessly throughout his life.

From early boyhood the author learned first-hand from teachers of the Ageless Wisdom. He has studied widely in world religions and philosophies. He is in addition an accomplished pianist, violinist, and cellist and plays many other instruments as well. His books, lectures, seminars, and music are inspiring and offer a true insight into the beauty of the Ageless Wisdom.

Torkom Saraydarian's books and music speak to the hearts and minds of a humanity eager for positive change. His books, covering a large spectrum of human existence, are written in straightforward, unpretentious, clear, and often humorous fashion. His works draw on personal experiences, varied and rich. He offers insight and explanations to anyone interested in applying spiritual guidelines to everyday life. His no-nonense approach is practical, simple, and readily accessible to anyone who is interested in finding real meaning in life.

Torkom Saraydarian has de-mystified the mysteries of the Ageless Wisdom. he has made the much needed link between the spiritual and the everyday worlds.

Look for exciting new books and music being released by Torkom Saraydarian.

Other Books by Torkom Saraydarian

The Ageless Wisdom
The Bhagavad Gita
Breakthrough to Higher Psychism
Challenge For Discipleship
Christ, The Avatar of Sacrificial Love
A Commentary on Psychic Energy
Cosmic Shocks
Cosmos in Man
Dialogue With Christ
Flame of Beauty, Culture, Love, Joy
The Flame of the Heart
Hiawatha and the Great Peace
The Hidden Glory of the Inner Man
I Was
Joy and Healing
Legend of Shamballa
New Dimensions in Healing
Other Worlds
The Psyche and Psychism
The Psychology of Cooperation and Group Consciousness
The Purpose of Life
The Science of Becoming Oneself
The Science of Meditation
The Sense of Responsibility in Society
Sex, Family, and the Woman in Society
The Solar Angel
Spiritual Regeneration
Symphony of the Zodiac
Talks on Agni
Triangles of Fire
Unusual Court
Woman, Torch of the Future
The Year 2000 & After

Vision Series Next Release: **The Mystery of Self-Image**

Booklets by
Torkom Saraydarian

Ordering Information

Write to the publisher for additional information regarding:

— Free catalog of author's books and music tapes

— Lecture tapes and videos

— Placement on mailing list

— New releases

Additional copies of *Dynamics of Success*

U.S. $8.95
Postage within U.S.A. $3.00
Plus applicable state sales tax

T.S.G. Publishing Foundation, Inc.
Visions for the Twenty-First Century
P.O. Box 4273
West Hills, California 91308
United States of America

TEL: (818) 888-7850
FAX: (818) 346-6457

These fine books have been published by the generous donations of the students of the Ageless Wisdom.

Our deep gratitude to all.